My Red Room

Written by Mario Scavatto
Illustrated by Anni Matsick

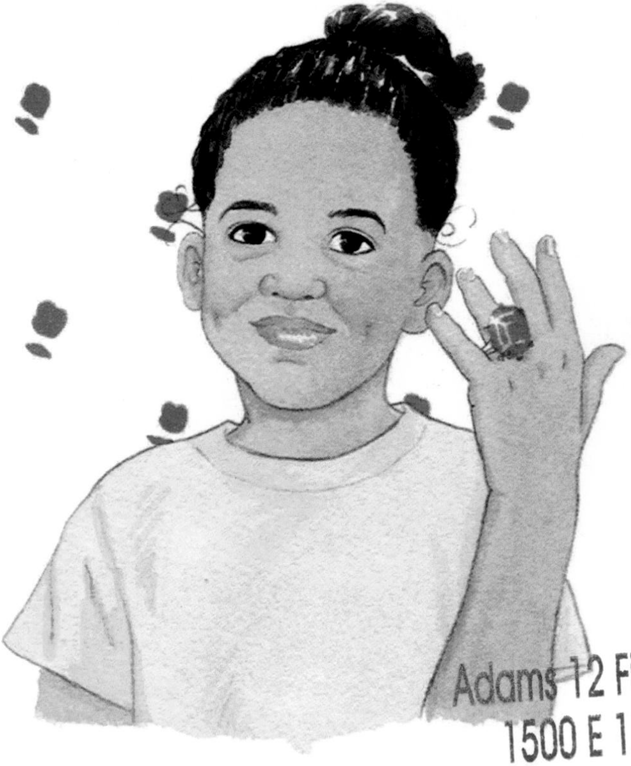

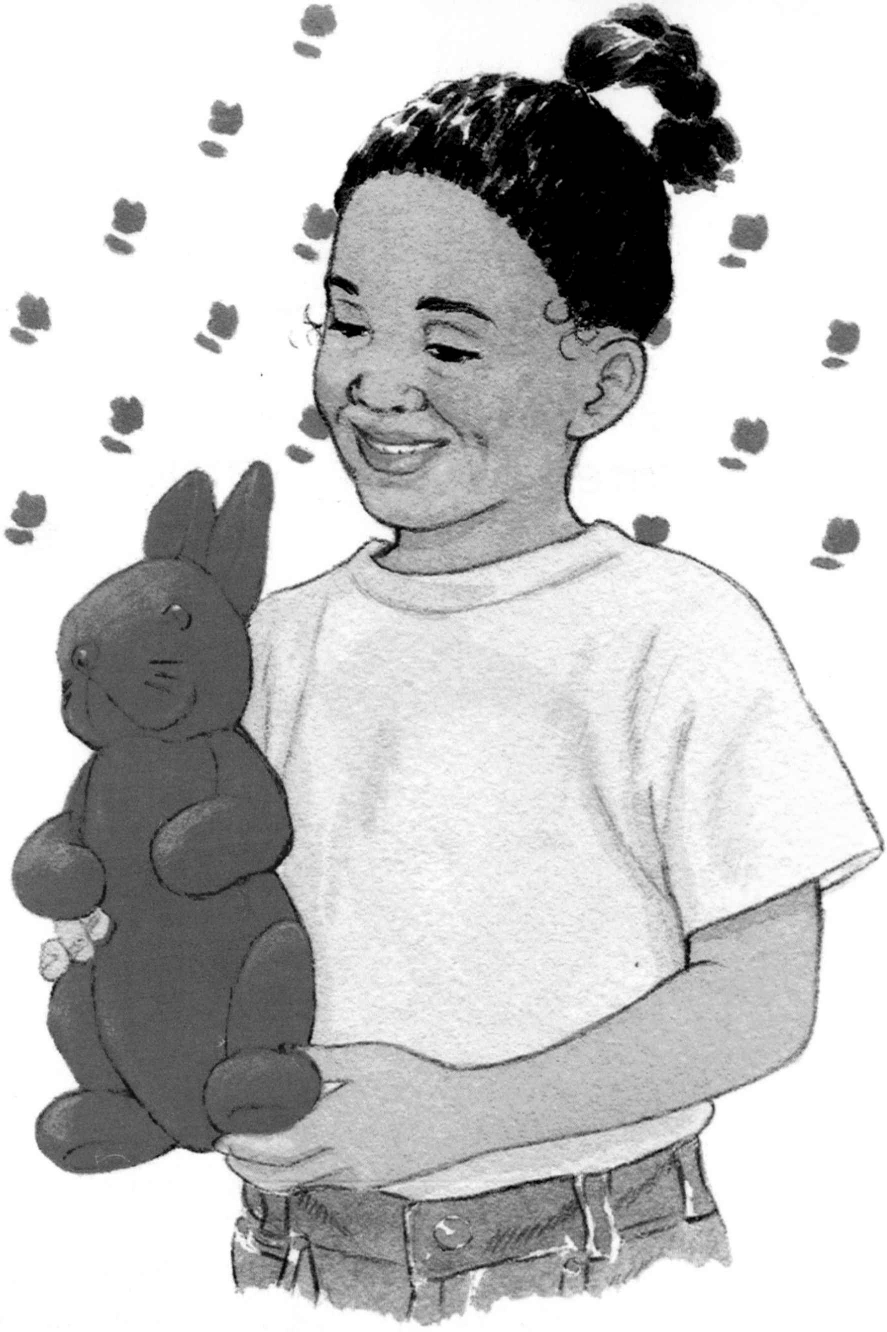

My red rabbit.

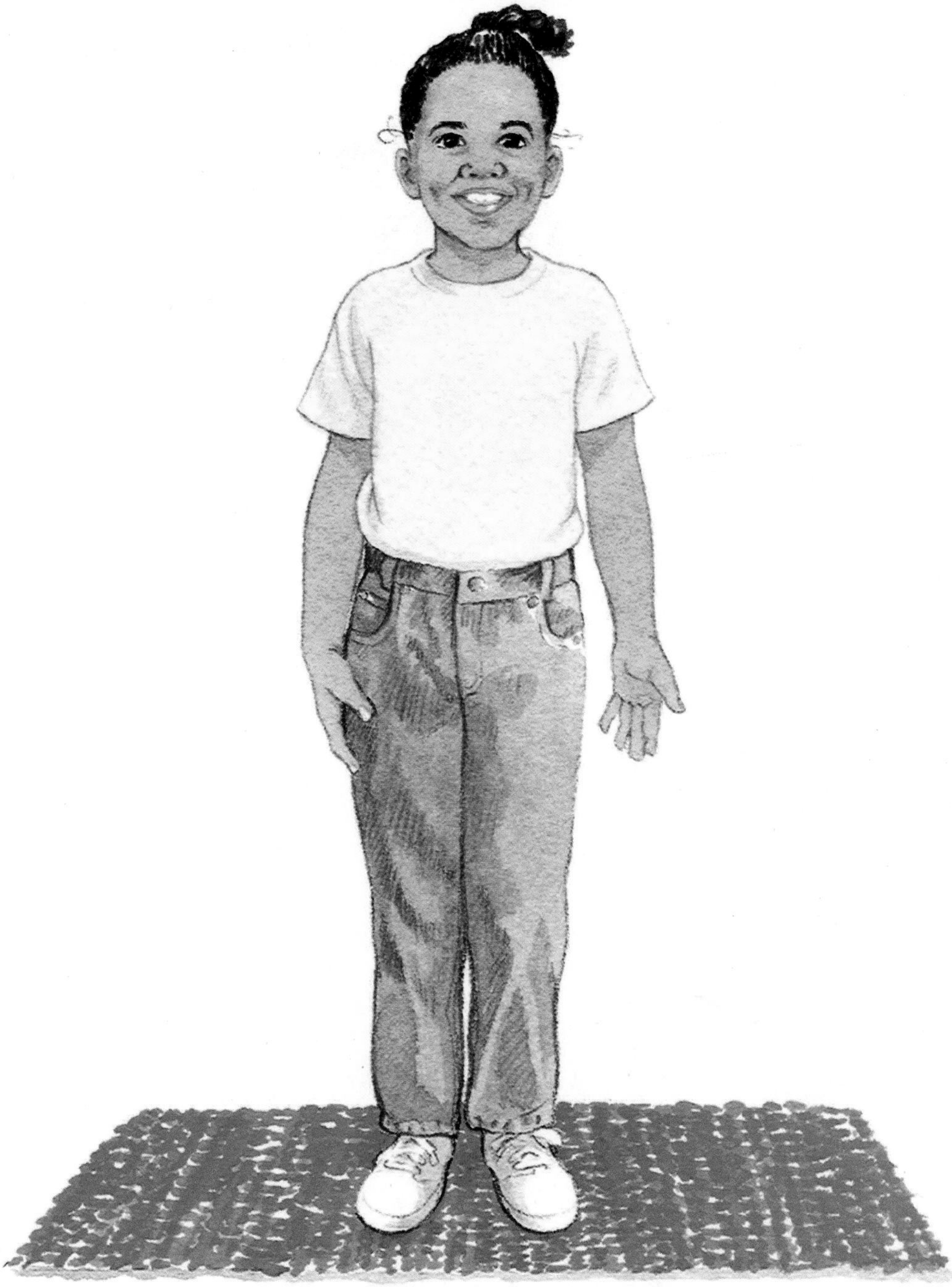

My red rug.

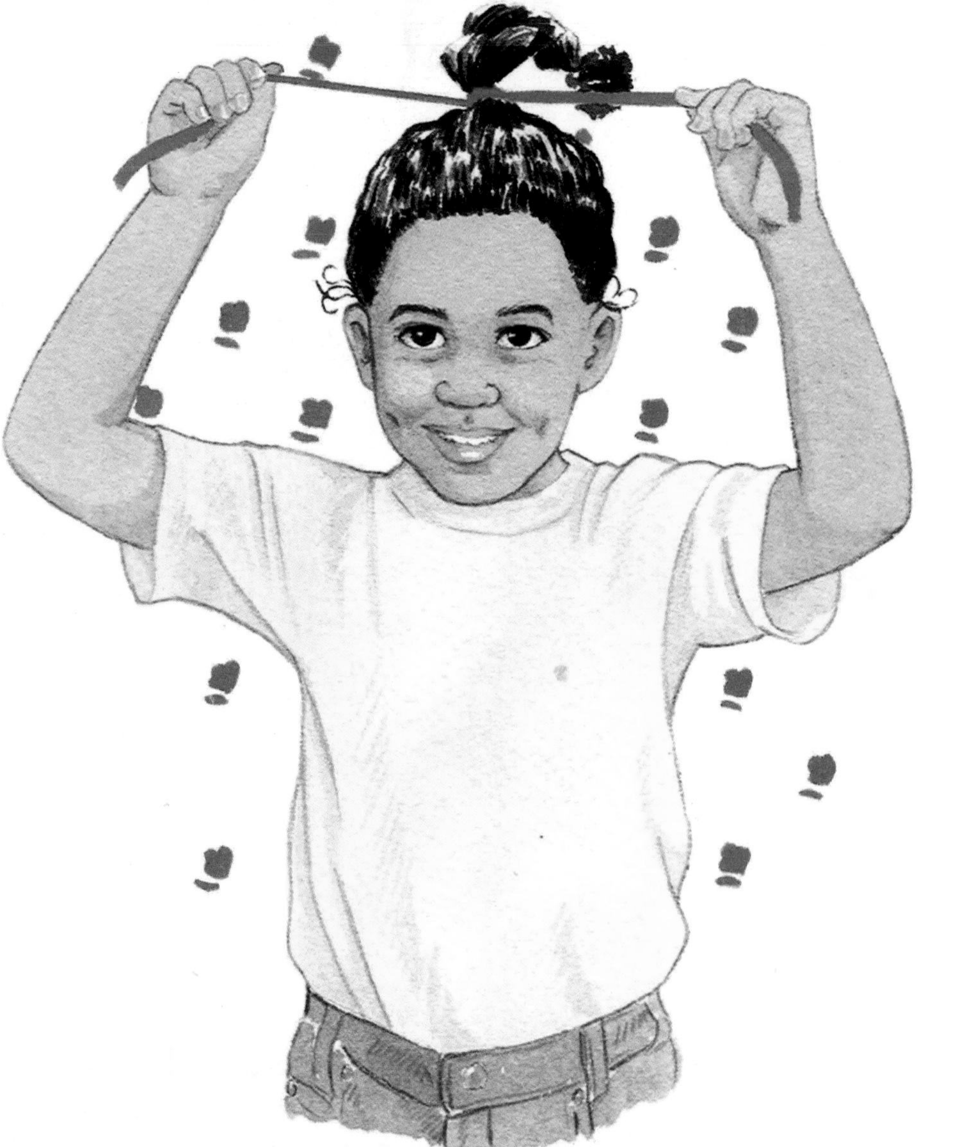

My red ribbon.

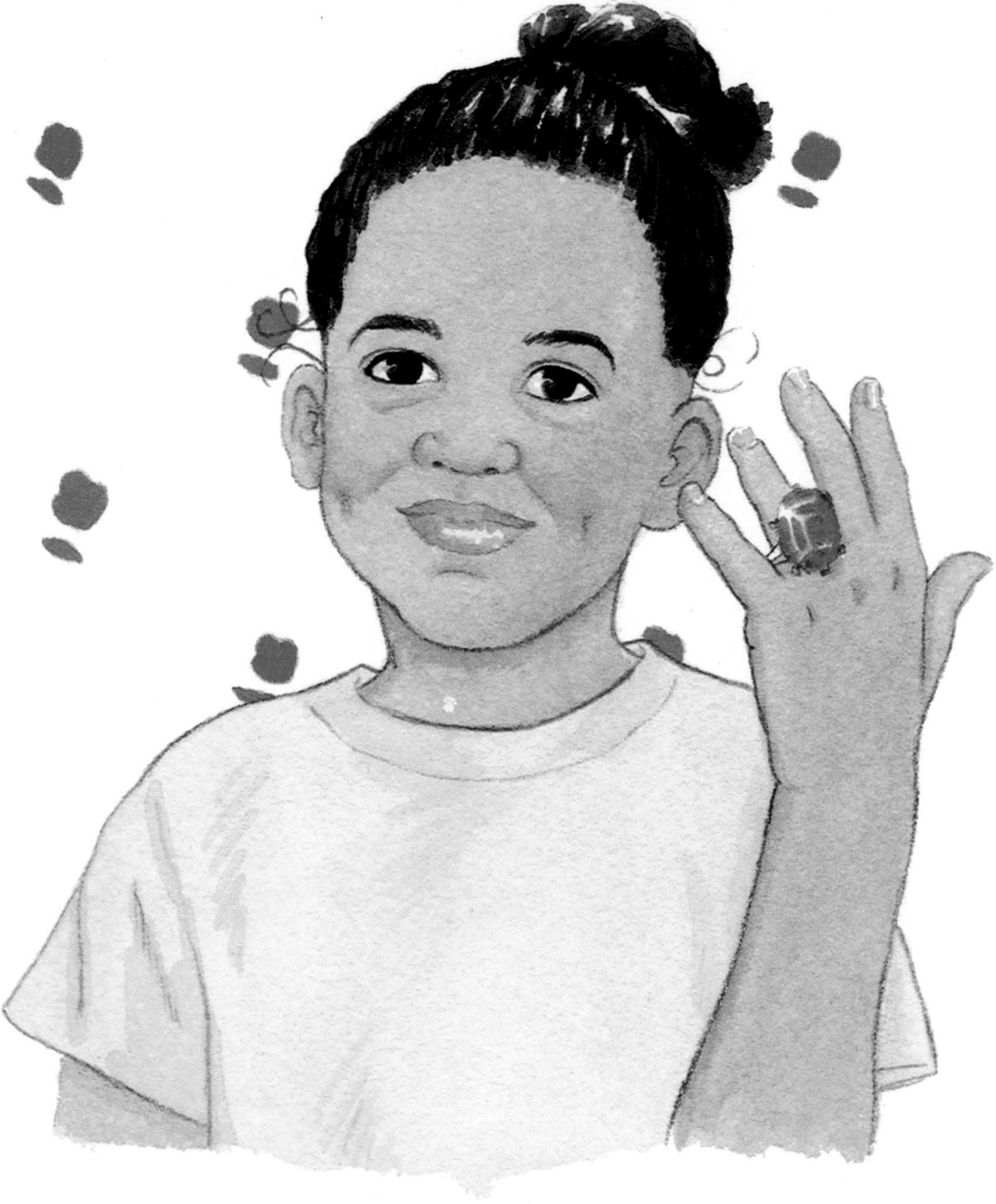

My red ring.

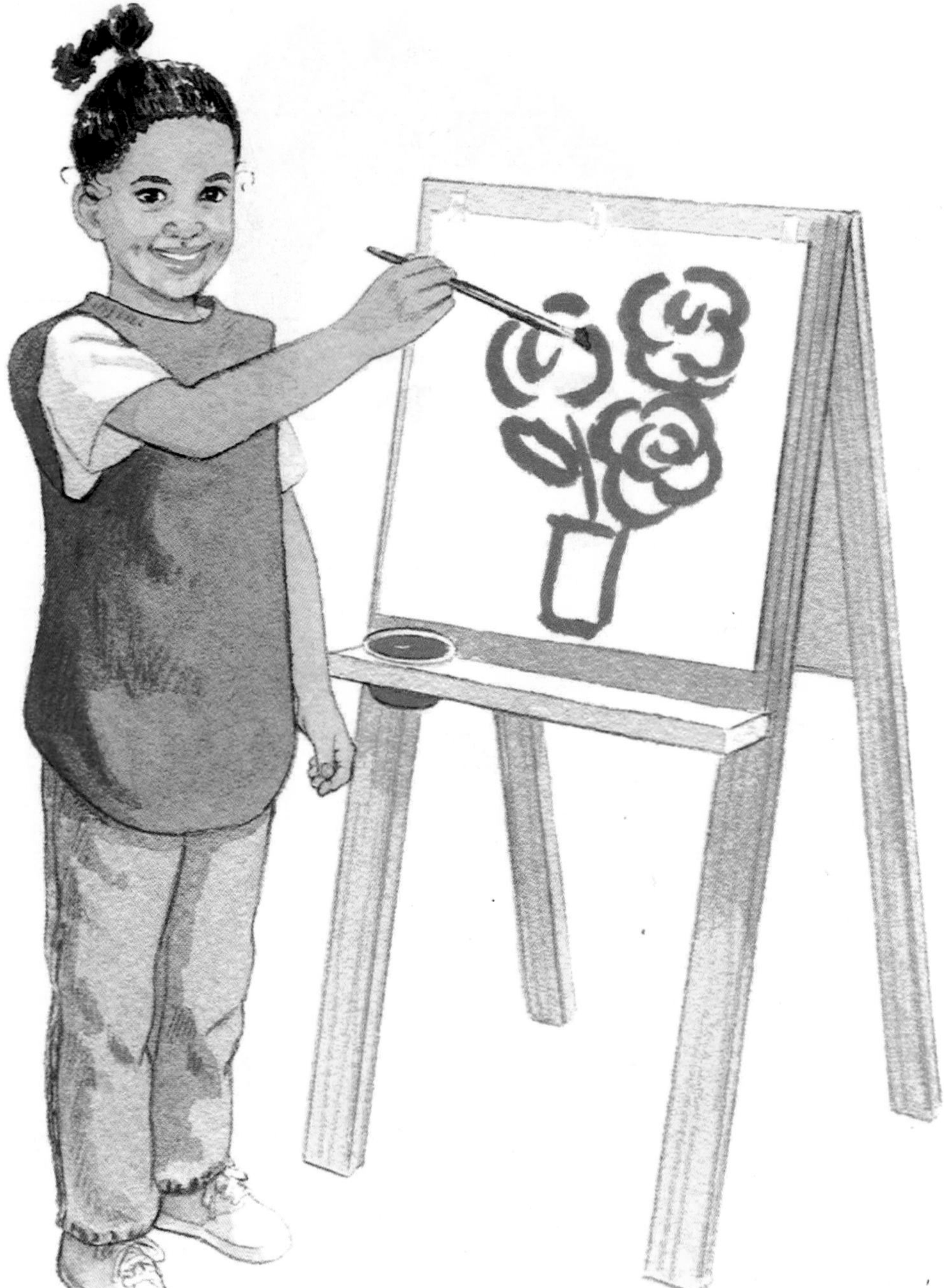

My red roses.

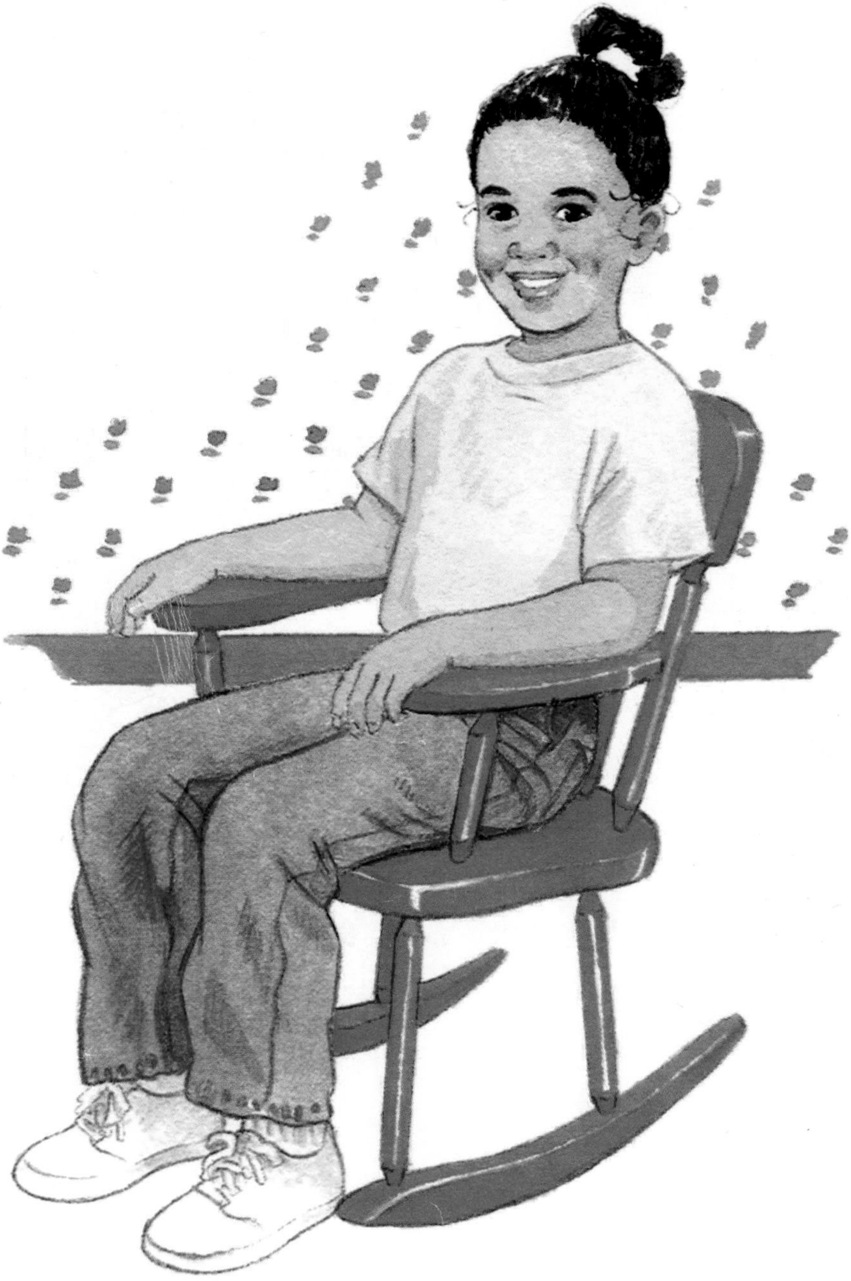

My red rocking chair.

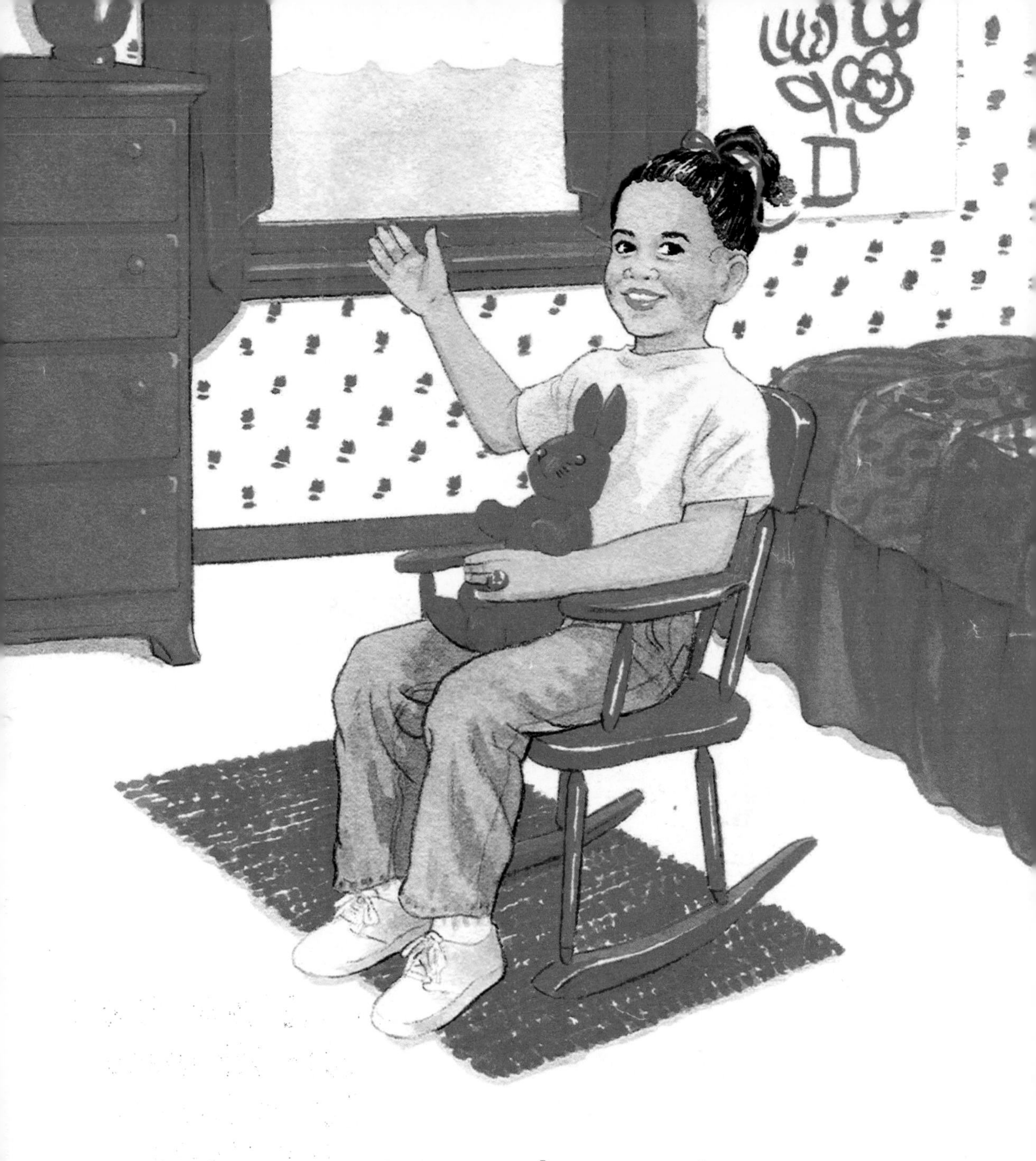

My red room!